A RESOURCE FROM

The Southern Baptist Theological Seminary

THE CALL TO MINISTRY

THIS WORKBOOK BELONGS TO:

IF FOUND, PLEASE CONTACT:

EMAIL   PHONE NUMBER

ISBN-13: 978-0615901039
ISBN-10: 0615901034

This is a different sort of book. Or workbook. Or journal. Whatever it is, it's meant to help you discern whether or not God has called you to ministry. And it's meant for you to use and devour. You'll notice pages with blank space; those pages are for you to respond to questions, react to the quotations and reflect on the Scripture references you'll find throughout.

So, open your Bible, get out your pen and discover whether God has called you to this most noble and weighty task.

> None but he who made the world can make a minister of the gospel.
>
> JOHN NEWTON

God calls all Christians to serve the cause of Christ and to proclaim the gospel. There are some people, though, whom God calls in a unique way for the purpose of serving the church as pastors, missionaries, church planters and ministers.

The evidence for such a call lies all over the New Testament. Paul says that Jesus himself gives to the church "shepherds and teachers" (Eph 4:11). In Acts 20:28, Paul tells the Ephesian elders to "pay careful attention to yourselves and to all the flock, in which the Holy Spirit has made you overseers." Again, in Matthew 9, Jesus tells his disciples to "pray earnestly to the Lord of the harvest to send out laborers into his harvest." It is the triune God himself who calls people to a life of service to him; such a task requires no less.

WHAT IS A CALLING?

Those who would deny
or minimize the fact that
God calls individual Christians
to special service must not only
discount the facts of human
experience but the evidence
of Scripture, which records the
calls of Moses, Isaiah, Jeremiah,
Paul and the commissioning
of the apostles.

R. KENT HUGHES

In the New Testament, the call was always to men to devote them-selves as much as possible to the preaching of the gospel so that the lost might be evangelized and the church strengthened. In today's terms, we would speak of this as a call to pastoral, church-planting, evangelistic or Bible-teaching ministry. Nowadays, there are countless other kinds of ministries on church staffs, the mission field, Christian organizations, etc., ministries to which people are guided by God. But here I am writing to those who are struggling with whether God is calling them to the "gos-pel ministry," that is, a ministry where their primary task is to preach the Word of God.

In summary, this call is God's planting the desire for vocational min-istry, and his persuading both the man and his Christian brothers and sisters that, when tested by Scripture, he has the qualifications which would reasonably point to proclaiming the gospel and building up the church as his work. The call to ministry has traditionally been divided into two categories: **THE INTERNAL CALL AND THE EXTERNAL CALL.**

THE INTERNAL CALL

THE EXTERNAL CALL

> For if I preach the gospel, that gives me no ground for boasting. For necessity is laid upon me. Woe to me if I do not preach the gospel!
>
> 1 CORINTHIANS 9:16

> The highest calling man can know is the call to the Christian ministry. Blessed is the man who feels in his heart the urge to preach the gospel.
>
> WILL HOUGHTON

THE INTERNAL CALL

BY R. ALBERT MOHLER JR.

How do you know if God is calling you?

First, there is an internal call. Through his Spirit, God speaks to those persons he has called to serve as pastors and ministers of his church. The great Reformer, Martin Luther, described this internal call as "God's voice heard by faith." Those whom God has called know this call by a sense of leading, purpose and growing commitment.

Charles Spurgeon identified the first sign of God's call to the ministry as "an intense, all-absorbing desire for the work." Those called by God sense a growing compulsion to preach and teach the Word, and to minister to the people of God.

This sense of compulsion should prompt the believer to consider whether God may be calling him to the ministry. Has God gifted you with the fervent desire to preach? Has he equipped you with the gifts necessary for ministry? Do you love God's Word and feel called to teach? Spurgeon warned those who sought his counsel not to preach if they could help it. "But," Spurgeon continued, "if he cannot help it, and he must preach or die, then he is the man." That sense of urgent commission is one of the central marks of an authentic call.

THE EXTERNAL CALL

Second, there is the external call. Baptists believe that God uses the congregation to "call out the called" to ministry. The congregation must evaluate and affirm the calling and gifts of the believer who feels called to the ministry. As a family of faith, the congregation should recognize and celebrate the gifts of ministry given to its members, and take responsibility to encourage those whom God has called to respond to that call with joy and submission.

These days, many persons think of careers rather than callings. The biblical challenge to "consider your call" should be extended from the call to salvation to the call to the ministry.

John Newton, famous for writing "Amazing Grace," once remarked: "None but he who made the world can make a minister of the gospel." Only God can call a true minister, and only he can grant the minister the gifts necessary for service. But the great promise of Scripture is that God does call ministers, and presents these servants as gifts to the church.

One key issue here is a common misunderstanding about the will of God. Some models of evangelical piety imply that God's will is something difficult for us to accept. We sometimes confuse this further by talking about "surrendering" to the will of God. As Paul makes clear in Romans 12:2, the will of God is good, worthy of eager acceptance and perfect. Those called by God to preach will be given a desire to preach as well as the gift of preaching. Beyond this, the God-called preacher will feel the same compulsion as the great apostle, who said, "Woe to me if I do not preach the gospel!" (1 Cor 9:16).

A CALL

TO

WHAT

?

Before addressing the issue of whether God has called someone to the ministry, there needs to be clarity regarding the kind of work the ministry includes. It's common for people to feel called to ministry when, in reality, their picture of ministry is a far cry from what the New Testament portrays.

The ministry is not to be entered into lightly. James says that "Not many of you should become teachers, my brothers, for you know that we who teach will be judged with greater strictness" (Jas 3:1). Similarly, the writer of Hebrews says that pastors "will have to give an account" to the Lord (Heb 13:17). God demands much of those who lead his people.

That's why it's imperative that those considering vocational ministry have a clear picture of what they're getting into.

SO LET'S CLEAR THINGS UP:

What is vocational ministry?

WHAT MINISTRY ISN'T

It's not easy.

Pastoral ministry is difficult. If you think ministry includes ease, down time and unlimited theological reading, you should reconsider. The demands of pastoral work don't stay within the confines of a normal work day, and the problems that pastors deal with don't always have answers in a text book. Beyond that, gospel ministers serve the Lord Jesus, who promised his disciples that the world will hate them (1 John 3:13; John 15:18-19). If you think life as an ambassador of Christ will be easy, remember how Jesus' contemporaries treated him, and remember that no servant is greater than his master (Matt 10:24; John 13:16; 15:20).

Virtually every day of his life,
the gospel minister will serve
in a context of constant challenges
to gospel truth and to biblical authority.
Many of these challenges will come
with an invitation, or perhaps a demand,
that the Christian leader compromise
his convictions and join the moral
revolution that is undeniably
taking place.

R. ALBERT MOHLER JR.

Do you feel a compulsion to follow Christ wherever he leads and whatever he requires? What limitations do you place on what you're willing to do for God?

But though we had already suffered and been shamefully treated at Philippi, as you know, we had boldness in our God to declare to you the gospel of God in the midst of much conflict.

1 THESSALONIANS 2:2

? How do you deal with difficult, selfish, sinful, critical people? Are you kind and compassionate?

> Ask yourselves again and again whether you would preach for Christ if you were sure to lay down your life for so doing? If you fear the displeasure of a man for doing your duty now, assure yourselves you are not yet thus minded.

GEORGE WHITEFIELD

Ministry is not a profession. It is a vocation. ... One must be called in order to do it. Although pastors may struggle with exactly what it means to be called by God to lead a church, they must have some sense that they are in ministry because God wants them to be. Time and again, amid the challenges of pastoral ministry, this divine, more-than-subjective authorization is a major means of pastoral preservation.

WILLIAM H. WILLIAMSON

Brethren, if the Lord gives you no zeal for souls, keep to the lapstone or the trowel, but avoid the pulpit.

C.H. SPURGEON

Today, it is fashionable in some circles to downplay the ministerial call. Some do this because they believe that the ministry is simply another profession like that of a lawyer or banker. They fail to realize that, while God calls his people to different walks of life, the ministry is uniquely exalted because it is a special call to the care and feeding of souls.

R. KENT HUGHES

The shepherds of the flock must realize they are stewards, not owners. Therefore, they serve as undershepherds of God's flock, subject to his rule.

MARK DEVER

You alone, as minsters of reconciliation, can give what the world with all its boasting and pride can never give — the infinite sweetness of the communion of the redeemed soul with the living God.

J. GRESHAM MACHEN

It's not just another job.

It should be true that a pastor would have excelled at whatever profession he entered, but that does not mean there is no difference between working as a lawyer or teacher and serving as a minister of the gospel. If you're considering the ministry, be sure you're not merely considering it as one option among many.

How do you view ministry in relation to other career options? Do you merely want to be in a helping profession? Do you view ministry merely as a means of personal fulfillment?

The aims of our ministry are eternal and spiritual. They are not shared by any of the professions.

JOHN PIPER

? Can you imagine doing anything other than ministry for the rest of your life? What would your life look like?

Advice frequently given is, "If you can avoid entering the ministry, do so! If you can do something else, do it!" This is sound counsel. If it is right for a man to give himself completely to the ministry of the gospel, he will feel that it is the only thing he can do.

DEREK PRIME AND ALISTAIR BEGG

> If you are more motivated by the awe-inspiring experience of having the esteem and respect of the people around you, you will do ministry in a way that is structured to get that respect.
>
> PAUL TRIPP

> We have nothing whereof to glory, and if we had, the very worst place in which to hang it out would be a pulpit; for there we are brought daily to feel our own insignificance and nothingness.
>
> C.H. SPURGEON

> Just as we have been approved by God to be entrusted with the gospel, so we speak, not to please man, but to please God"
>
> 1 THESSALONIANS 2:4

It's not for fame.

The apostle Paul warns against thinking that "godliness is a means of gain" (1 Tim 6:5). Elsewhere, he rebuked the Corinthians for aligning with certain men, telling them that God has ordered things so that no one may boast except in the Lord (1 Cor 1:18-31). God himself has declared that he will not share his glory with another (Isa 42:8; 48:11). The goal of ministry is not to be a conference speaker or a best-selling author. For the apostle Paul, ministry was not about making much of himself: "I do not account my life of any value nor as precious to myself, if only I may finish my course and the ministry that I received from the Lord Jesus, to testify to the gospel of the grace of God" (Acts 20:24).

If glory is your goal, you're not called to the ministry.

Are you envisioning your ministry becoming like the ministry of one of your heroes with wide influence, or can you be truly content to be faithful and honor Christ in small things? What do you hope to accomplish in your ministry?

"The pulpit is never
to be the ladder
by which ambition
is to climb."

C.H. SPURGEON

A good indicator that a man is called into ministry is that he will, with some proper hesitation but certain determination, take the path of shattered dreams, trusting God to replace them with better ones. What might it look like to seek the fame of another at the "loss" of your own?

> Do I still want to be
> a pastor if I never
> write a book, never
> speak at a confer-
> ence and never have
> a big church? Our
> passion must be to
> feed the flock, not
> feed our egos.
>
> KEVIN DEYOUNG 🔊

WHAT
MINISTRY
IS

It's for God's glory

Ministry is about God. Paul says that his ministry — and his willingness to be given over to death — was for Jesus' sake (2 Cor 4:7-11). He ministered in the hope that, as grace extended to more and more people, it would increase thanksgiving, to the glory of God (2 Cor 4:15). A desire to be faithful to God and to his Word — rather than a desire to please people or be innovative — must drive all that a pastor does. The pastor's primary task is faithfulness to God, for it is the glory of God that supplies purpose and meaning to all of life and ministry.

Pastoral ministry
is more than caring
for people. It is worship.
It must be pursued
as worship, because
Jesus really is everything.

RAY ORTLUND JR.

In 1979, John Piper considered leaving his teaching post at Bethel College to enter the ministry. His dad, Bill Piper, was an evangelist with abundant experience in many kinds of churches. Bill Piper knew what awaited anyone entering the ministry. He wrote his son a letter, wanting him to have a clear picture of what the pastorate entails. Here is what he said:

"Now I want you to remember a few things about the pastorate. Being a pastor today involves more than merely teaching and preaching. You'll be the comforter of the fatherless and the widow. You'll counsel constantly with those whose homes and hearts are broken. You'll have to handle divorce problems and a thousand marital situations. You'll have to exhort and advise young people involved in sordid and illicit sex, with drugs and violence. You'll have to visit the hospitals, the shut-ins, the elderly. A mountain of problems will be laid on your shoulders and at your doorstep.

And then there's the heartache of ministering to a weak and carnal and worldly, apathetic group of professing Christians, very few of whom will be found trustworthy and dependable.

Then there are a hundred administrative responsibilities as pastor. You're the generator and sometimes the janitor. The church will look to you for guidance in building programs, church growth, youth activities, outreach, extra services, etc. You'll be called upon to arbitrate all kinds of problems. At times you will feel the weight of the world on your shoulders. Many pastors have broken under the strain.

If the Lord has called you, these things will not deter nor dismay you. But I wanted you to know the whole picture. As in all of our Lord's work there will be a thousand compensations. You'll see that people trust Christ as Savior and Lord. You'll see these grow in the knowledge of Christ and his Word. You'll witness saints enabled by your preaching to face all manner of tests. You'll see God at work in human lives, and there is no joy comparable to this.

Just ask yourself, son, if you are prepared not only to preach and teach, but also to weep over men's souls, to care for the sick and dying and to bear the burdens carried today by the saints of God."

— *Bill Piper*

In summary, ministry isn't about you. It's about God, it's about caring for his people and about proclaiming the gospel of Jesus Christ.

John the Baptist was willing to decrease so that Christ might increase (John 3:29-30). Are you most concerned with God's glory? What about ministry is most attractive to you?

> For am I now seeking the approval of man, or of God? Or am I trying to please man? If I were still trying to please man, I would not be a servant of Christ.
>
> GALATIANS 1:10

"But I do not account my life of any value nor as precious to myself, if only I may finish my course and the ministry that I received from the Lord Jesus, to testify to the gospel of the grace of God."

ACTS 20:24

Shepherd the flock of God that is among you, exercising oversight, not under compulsion, but willingly, as God would have you; not for shameful gain, but eagerly; not domineering over those in your charge, but being examples to the flock. And when the chief Shepherd appears, you will receive the unfading crown of glory.

1 PETER 5:2-4

The whole of our ministry must be carried on in tender love to our people. We must let them see that nothing pleaseth us but what profiteth them.

RICHARD BAXTER

Christ loved the souls of men, and had so great a regard to their salvation, that he thought it worthy for him so to lay out himself. Shall not his ministers and servants be willing to do the same?

JONATHAN EDWARDS

If we are afflicted, it is for your comfort and salvation; and if we are comforted, it is for your comfort, which you experience when you patiently endure the same sufferings that we suffer.

2 CORINTHIANS 1:6

It's for the good of God's people.

How do ministers glorify God in ministry? By pouring themselves out for the souls God entrusts to them. Paul says that "I will most gladly spend and be spent for your souls" (2 Cor 12:15). God gave pastors and teachers "to equip the saints for the work of ministry, for building up the body of Christ" (Eph 4:12). There is no higher calling than to care for God's people, even at the expense of your life. Pastors follow after the model of Christ, who gave his own life, "and we ought to lay down our lives for the brothers" (1 John 3:16).

To what extent are you willing to spend and be spent for the sake of God's people (2 Cor 12:15)?

Even if I am to be poured out as a drink offering upon the sacrificial offering of your faith, I am glad and rejoice with you all.

PHILIPPIANS 2:17

Now I rejoice in my
sufferings for your
sake, and in my flesh
I am filling up what is
lacking in Christ's
afflictions for the sake
of his body, that is,
the church.

COLOSSIANS 1:24

> We are ambassadors for Christ, God making his appeal through us. We implore you on behalf of Christ, be reconciled to God.
>
> 2 CORINTHIANS 5:20

> I charge you in the presence of God and of Christ Jesus, who is to judge the living and the dead, and by his appearing and his kingdom: preach the word; be ready in season and out of season; reprove, rebuke, and exhort, with complete patience and teaching.
>
> 2 TIMOTHY 4:1-2

> We are seeking to uphold the world, to save it from the curse of God, to perfect the creation, to attain the ends of Christ's death, to save ourselves and others from damnation, to overcome the devil and demolish his kingdom, to set up the kingdom of Christ and to attain and help others to the kingdom of glory.
>
> RICHARD BAXTER

> I count it the highest honor that God can confer on any man to call him to be a herald of the gospel.
>
> D. MARTYN LLOYD-JONES

It's for the advance of the gospel.

The apostle Paul, from inside his prison cell, encouraged the Philippians that "what has happened to me has really served to advance the gospel, so that it has become known throughout the whole imperial guard and to all the rest that my imprisonment is for Christ" (Phil 1:12-13). He was willing to endure imprisonment if it meant that the gospel would advance. He knew that "the word of God is not bound," even if he was (2 Tim 2:9).

The gospel must comprise the content of the pastor's ministry, for the gospel alone is God's power for salvation. The Book of Acts tells the story of the church's growth, which resulted from the Word of the Lord increasing and going forth (Acts 6:7; 12:24; 19:20). As the Word went forth, the church was built. That was Jesus' plan for the early church, and it hasn't changed.

I am astonished that you are so quickly deserting him who called you in the grace of Christ and are turning to a different gospel — not that there is another one, but there are some who trouble you and want to distort the gospel of Christ. But even if we or an angel from heaven should preach to you a gospel contrary to the one we preached to you, let him be accursed. As we have said before, so now I say again: If anyone is preaching to you a gospel contrary to the one you received, let him be accursed.

GALATIANS 1:6-9

Jesus came and said to them, "All authority
in heaven and on earth has been given to me.
Go therefore and make disciples of all
nations, baptizing them in the name of the
Father and of the Son and of the Holy Spirit,
teaching them to observe all that I have com-
manded you. And behold, I am with you
always, to the end of the age."

MATTHEW 28:18-20

ARE YOU CALLED?

— DESIRE —

Part of the internal call is aspiration, that is, an irrepressible desire to engage in the work of the ministry. The imperative presence of this compulsion is reflected in 1 Tim 3:1, "It is a trustworthy statement: if any man aspires to the office of overseer, it is a fine work he desires to do."

This may also be termed a "secret call," since this desire often begins to grow long before others recognize the person as a candidate for ministry. Some people first become aware of the call originating through their reading of the Bible. Many recall the powerful effect of a sermon or a book that initiated their sense of summons. Others will refer to the influence or example of a minister they admired. Regardless of the means through which God began to awaken you to his purpose, your encounters with the Scriptures should continually nourish and affirm the secret call.

So the internal call should be a continuing aspiration. Without choosing to think about it you find it keeps surfacing in your thoughts. The more you wish to ignore the possibility that God is calling you, the more preoccupied you become with it.

This aspiration for the gospel ministry is also self-sacrificing. You feel drawn to preach God's Word, not for what it will do for you, but because you long to glorify God through the proclamation of his gospel, the conversion of souls and the building up of his church.

How have others described this desire for ministry?

This steadfast and divinely implanted desire to labor for souls is substantially what is meant by the 'internal call.' In the man truly called, it grows, it increases. As he reflects on it, and prays about it, the great salvation becomes greater and nearer to him than when he first believed. The man is made to feel that for him all other avocations are trifling, and worldly employ-ments unattractive.

BASIL MANLY JR.

We must feel that woe is unto us if we preach not the gospel; the word of God must be unto us as fire in our bones, other-wise, if we undertake the ministry, we shall be unhappy in it, shall be unable to bear the self-denials incident to it, and shall be of little service to those among whom we minister.

C.H. SPURGEON

The man who is once moved by the Spirit of God to this work will prefer it to thousands of gold and silver; so that, though he is at times intimidated by a sense of its importance and difficulty, compared with his own great insufficiency (for it is to be presumed a call of this sort, if indeed from God, will be accompanied with humility and self-abasement), yet he cannot give it up.

JOHN NEWTON

A true call often comes with an insatiable desire to, at all costs, serve God and his people. There is a strong sense in the heart that it is ministry or nothing else ... The called man cannot imagine going into another vocation: he daydreams about ministry, he talks about ministry, and he cannot wait to be in ministry. There is an abiding, relentless desire for the work of ministry that the called man cannot shake off or ignore — even amidst hardship, persecution, and fear.

DARRIN PATRICK

The secret call means the good testimony of our heart, that we undertake the offered office [not] from ... any selfish feeling but from a sincere fear of God.

JOHN CALVIN

Some people have mistaken zeal or ambition — even for something good — as a genuine desire for the ministry. Donald S. Whitney lists ten things that should not be mistaken for a call to ministry:

Ambition to be noticed, to prove yourself or to make a difference;

Confidence that you could do well in the ministry;

Compassion for hurting people;

Confusion about a mystical experience;

Fluency in public speaking;

Knowledge of the Bible;

Failure at all other types of work;

Belief that ministry would be the best means to an easy life, study and intellectual pursuits or wealth;

Acquiescence to the expectation of a parent or the selfish opinion of others; and

Conviction that the church needs you.

**DO NOT ENTER THE MINISTRY
IF ONE OF THE PRECEEDING ITEMS
IS YOUR MAIN MOTIVATION.**

YOU MUST
BE CALLED.

How does your desire compare to Whitney's list of things not to be mistaken for a call?

1

Ambition to be noticed, to prove yourself or to make a difference;

2

Confidence that you could do well in the ministry;

(3)

Compassion for
hurting people;

(4)

Confusion about
a mystical
experience;

(5)

Fluency in
public speaking;

6

Knowledge of
the Bible;

7

Failure at all
other types
of work;

8

Belief that minis-
try would be the
best means to an
easy life, study
and intellectual
pursuits or wealth;

9

Acquiescence to the expectation of a parent or the selfish opinion of others; and

10

Conviction that the church needs you.

How long have you felt a desire to enter the ministry?
Where did it originate?

How does your desire compare to that described by Spurgeon, Newton, Manly and others (on page 53)?

QUALIFI

CATIONS ——

Do your best
to present yourself
to God as one approved,
a worker who has no need
to be ashamed, rightly
handling the word
of truth.

2 TIMOTHY 2:15

Who is sufficient for
these things? For we are not,
like so many, peddlers of God's
word, but as men of sincerity,
as commissioned by God,
in the sight of God we speak
in Christ.

2 CORINTHIANS 2:16

BY DANIEL S. DUMAS

If you have the earnest desire to enter the ministry, and you can see your-self doing nothing else, the next step is to evaluate your qualifications.

Nobody is sufficient for these things, yet God chooses to use imperfect people for the task of reconciling sinners to himself anyway. And he requires certain characteristics for those he calls. The good of those under authority depends on the faithfulness of those in authority. God gave pastors to lead the church, and if pastors are unfaithful in their lives and leadership, their people suffer. God cares about the holiness of all his people, but he is emphatic about the character of those who lead his people.

Paul gives a list of qualifications for church eldership in 1 Timothy 3:1-7, and almost all of the qualifications have to do with character. Paul's list is not exhaustive, but it still gives an opportunity for elders and those aspiring to eldership to examine themselves against the brilliant light of Scripture.

Elders are not required to abide by a stricter moral code than other Christians, but there are unique repercussions if their morality fails. In other words, there isn't a higher standard for the character of elders, but there is a higher accountability.

Paul insists on an elder's holiness in five major life categories: public, marital, family, personal and doctrinal. Paul sums up these areas with two words: above reproach. This is Paul's way of saying that the elder should have no loop-holes in his character. Being above reproach means you have unimpeachable character, but it doesn't mean you're flawless.

1 TIMOTHY 3:1-7

The saying is trustworthy: If anyone aspires to the office of overseer, he desires a noble task. Therefore an overseer must be above reproach, the husband of one wife, sober-minded, self-controlled, respectable, hospitable, able to teach, not a drunkard, not violent but gentle, not quarrelsome, not a lover of money. He must manage his own household well, with all dignity keeping his children submissive, for if someone does not know how to manage his own household, how will he care for God's church? He must not be a recent convert, or he may become puffed up with conceit and fall into the condemnation of the devil. Moreover, he must be well thought of by outsiders, so that he may not fall into disgrace, into a snare of the devil.

How do you measure up to Paul's list of qualifications?

HUSBAND OF ONE WIFE

V.2

FOR FURTHER STUDY

Ephesians 5:25-33

The first qualification for leadership in the local church is not charisma, not visionary leadership, not captivating oration. The first qualification is faithfulness, and the first place to look for this is a man's marriage. You won't be a faithful elder if you aren't first a faithful husband. If you're single, the same faithfulness demanded in marriage needs to be a mark of your singleness. How do you measure up?

SOBER-MINDED

V.2

FOR FURTHER STUDY

1 Peter 4:7

Sober-mindedness is a disposition that gives serious attention to one's doctrine and life. If you're an elder, or want to be an elder, you need to take seriously not only your doctrine and life, but how it makes an impact on those under your leadership.

If you want to be in ministry, you need to cultivate sober-mindedness in all aspects of your life. You need to cultivate moderation in your life rather than excess. You need to be sensible in your decisions rather than rash and impulsive. You need to make a habit of mature, clear and serious thinking rather than having bouts of boyish, immature, frat-boy kinds of behavior and thought. When you were a child, you could speak and think and reason as such, but as a man, you need to put away childish ways, and think like the sober-minded man God created you to be, and that God's people need you to be.

SELF-CONTROLLED

V.2

FOR FURTHER STUDY

1 Corinthians 9:24-27

Self-control is a big deal in Paul's mind. It's the final fruit of the Spirit listed in Galatians 5:22-23. Paul isn't the only one who deemed it important, the Book of Proverbs also warns that, "A man without self-control is like a city broken into and left without walls" (Prov 25:28). In a culture where indulging any and all desires is encouraged, it is imperative that your people see you practice and display self-mastery. Richard Baxter says that "self-denial is of absolute necessity in every Christian, but it is doubly necessary in a minister, as without it he cannot do God an hour's faithful service."

"If a man cannot control his life when he is alone, he does not belong in the pastorate. If he is the kind of person who needs to have a committee to keep him in line, he will end up bringing grief to the church."

JOHN MACARTHUR

RESPECTABLE

V.2

FOR
FURTHER
STUDY

2 Corinthians 4:2

Every man craves respect, whether it's from his wife, his boss, his children or his dog. But if you aspire to be in ministry, you need to spend less time making sure everyone around you gives you the respect you think you deserve, and spend more time living a life that demands it. Put order and discipline into your life. Exercise dominion in the areas God has entrusted to you.

HOSPITABLE

V.2

FOR FURTHER STUDY

Hebrews 13:1-2

As an elder and pastor, your home should be a place of respite, a place where faith is strengthened, where fellow Christians and traveling missionaries can rest.

Your home isn't only for Christians, it should also be a place where skeptics and sinners come and witness the gospel in action. You need to love your wife and raise your children in a way that commends the gospel to those in your home. This doesn't mean your family life is perfect, or your house is a show room, but you're still called to use your home and resources to bless Christians, unbelievers and strangers (1 Pet 4:9).

ABLE TO TEACH

V.2

FOR FURTHER STUDY

Titus 1:9

The ability to teach is a unique requirement for elders. A man of stellar character can be disqualified by an inability to teach. He should not only be able to teach clearly the doctrines of the faith, but also defend the church against false teaching (Titus 1:9). When pastors "contend for the faith that was once for all delivered to the saints" (Jude 3), they must be able to articulate and refute, to contend and defend, in season and out of season.

NOT A DRUNKARD

V.2

FOR FURTHER STUDY

Proverbs 20:1

It seems obvious, but pastors can't be drunkards. God commands that all Christians "not get drunk with wine ... but be filled with the Spirit" (Eph 5:18). You can't be mastered by both wine and the Spirit; it's one or the other. Remember, your people are looking to you for an example of how to walk in a manner worthy of the gospel.

"Maybe you love people, but you don't know how to correct them in a truly gentle way, without harshness, without hurting. If so, find someone who can serve as a model and teacher for you in this area; it is tremendously important. And, for the sake of our Lord Jesus Christ and for the love of his sheep, stay out of the pastorate until you have learned."

JOHN FRAME

NOT VIOLENT BUT GENTLE

V.3

FOR FURTHER STUDY

Matthew 11:28-29

As an elder, you can't get into physical altercations with your people when they irritate you. If you've got a short fuse and your frustration comes with physical manifestations, then you're not qualified to shepherd the flock. When your sheep bite, you can't bite back.

Your gentleness needs to be visible in your instruction of others. Model yourself after Paul, who entreated the Corinthians "by the meekness and gentleness of Christ," (2 Cor 10:1), and who told Timothy to correct his opponents "with gentleness" (2 Tim 2:25).

Gentleness also needs to be visible when you receive criticism. Do you become defensive when you receive criticism, or do you respond with humility and an honest belief that "faithful are the wounds of a friend" (Prov 27:6)?

Whether you're receiving criticism, or you're teaching, refuting, rebuking, defending and training in righteousness, it all needs to be laden with gentleness.

NOT QUARRELSOME

V.3

FOR FURTHER STUDY

2 Timothy 2:24-25

Elders are called to refute false teachers, but they are not called to go around looking for a fight. Do you love to argue? Do you love to be right? Do you love to argue until everyone thinks you're right? If so, then marvel at the Lord Jesus, who never engaged in debate for the sake of debating or belittling others. He only ever opened his mouth for the purpose of teaching, leading and shepherding. Even in his harshest rebukes, he had in mind the good of those around him. Elder, protect the flock, but don't go around looking for wolves to fight.

NOT A LOVER OF MONEY

V.3

FOR FURTHER STUDY

Matthew 6:19-21

Some people think that being in ministry, with the simple lifestyle that often comes with it, will render a love of money irrelevant. But that's not so. You can simultaneously be poor and greedy.

If you struggle with greed, you need to give more. The best way to stop loving money is to attack it with aggressive generosity. Your money is not your own. You can't call your people to lay up treasures in heaven while you're anxious about building and protecting yours on earth.

MANAGING HIS OWN HOUSEHOLD

V.4

FOR FURTHER STUDY

Deuteronomy 6:4-9

There is no better way to examine a man's leadership qualities and evaluate the long-term results of his leadership than to enter his home. The home is a microcosm of the church, and if you can't pastor the people in your home, you won't be able to pastor the people in your church. If your wife is hesitant about your fitness for ministry then you should be, too. If you "succeed" at church but fail at home, then you fail. Period.

"Christ has not only ordained that there shall be such officers in his church — he has not only specified their duties and prerogatives — but he gives the requisite qualifications, and calls those thus qualified, and by that call gives them their official authority."

CHARLES HODGE

NOT A NOVICE

V.6

FOR FURTHER STUDY

2 Peter 1:5-8

The elder is called to exposit and apply the Scriptures to the lives of his people, and the ability to do that develops and deepens with time and practice. The longer a man walks with God and trusts him through trials, the more apt that man will be to speak truth into people's lives. It takes time for trials to result in a faith tested with genuineness (1 Pet 1:6-7).

WELL THOUGHT OF BY OUTSIDERS

V.7

FOR FURTHER STUDY

1 Thessalonians 4:9-12

The list of qualifications began with the call to be above reproach, and like a bookend, it ends with a call to be above reproach to those outside the church. An elder must have good rapport with unbelievers in the community. If you don't live that way, you're leading yourself into a snare of the devil (1 Tim 3:7).

If you plan to be well thought of by outsiders, your life needs to match your role as an elder. You better know where your weaknesses lie because the devil most certainly does. Keep close watch on and attack those weaknesses. If you don't, those little inconsistencies will become chains that bind you and may eventually disqualify you.

RICHARD BAXTER'S

EIGHT REASONS A PASTOR SHOULD CARE ABOUT CHARACTER

Richard Baxter was an English Puritan preacher and author of *The Reformed Pastor*. In the book, he lists eight reasons pastors need to watch their lives closely.

4

People are watching you,
and they'll be there
to observe your fall;

———

1

You have heaven
to win or lose;

———

2

You're depraved with sinful
inclinations;

———

3

You're exposed to greater
temptations than others;

———

5

There's more hypocrisy
involved when you sin;

———

6

Your work requires more
grace than others;

———

7

The honor of Christ lies on
you more than on others; and

———

8

The success of your labors
depends on it.

———

— GIFTS —

If you — and those around you — believe you're qualified for church leadership, the next step is to undergo an honest evaluation of your fitness for the work. The first part of this evaluation is to ask yourself whether you have the required gifts and abilities.

In the same way that someone with a severe aversion to blood is not likely called to be a surgeon, there are some natural gifts that may indicate whether you're called to the ministry. The apostle Peter told his readers, "As each has received a gift, use it to serve one another, as good stewards of God's varied grace" (1 Pet 4:10). For you to use your gifts to serve the body of Christ, you need to know what gifts you do and do not have.

You can be sure that, if God has called you, he will equip you with the necessary gifts and abilities. You might not possess all the necessary gifts immediately, but it is still wise to identify which gifts you possess, which gifts you lack and which gifts you need to cultivate further.

One aspect of the external, or public, side of God's call to the preaching ministry is confirmation by others. As your fellow Christians observe your life and service, and compare what they see with the scriptural qualifications for ministry, the Holy Spirit bears witness to them that God has called you, and they tell you so.

DONALD S. WHITNEY

What are your gifts?

John Calvin cited humility and contentment as requisite for ministry:

"They who are called to preach the gospel, to teach the flock of our Lord Jesus Christ and to lead them, cannot do their duty unless they lay all ambition aside and seek not to please men, not to be seen, nor to be in reputation. They must account all this as vanity, and content themselves to build the church, to procure the salvation of souls, to magnify the majesty of our Lord Jesus and cause all to submit themselves obediently to God. To be short, let it suffice them to put forth the simplicity of the gospel, to enrich those who desire to be satisfied with God's blessings. Let them content themselves herein, and not covet as many do to be exalted, to be esteemed for their showy babbling and lofty speech, for their subtleties, for their fine and sharp wits, for their fleeting, pretentious displays. All these things must be laid underfoot, or else we can never serve God and his church."

Martin Luther listed eight qualities necessary for a minister:

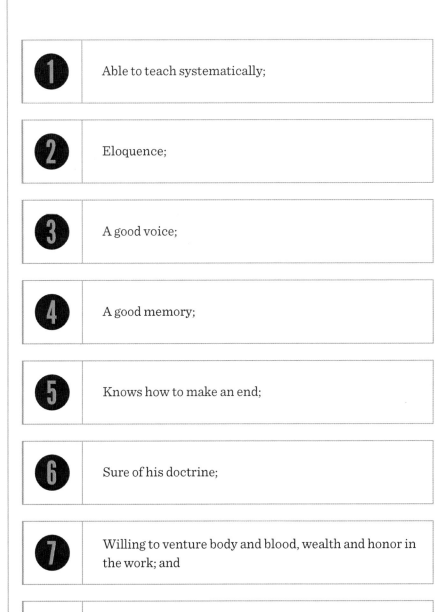

1. Able to teach systematically;

2. Eloquence;

3. A good voice;

4. A good memory;

5. Knows how to make an end;

6. Sure of his doctrine;

7. Willing to venture body and blood, wealth and honor in the work; and

8. Suffers himself to be mocked and jeered by everyone.

LUTHER ALSO SAID:

"Men who hold the office of the ministry should have the heart of a mother toward the church. Unless your heart toward the sheep is like that of a mother toward her children — a mother who walks through fire to save her children — you will not be fit to be a preacher. Labor, work, unthankfulness, hatred, envy and all kinds of sufferings will meet you in this office. If, then, the mother heart, the great love, is not there to drive the preachers, the sheep will be poorly served."

1.

Do I like to teach all kinds of people in all kinds of settings?

Kevin DeYoung asks these questions regarding gifts and inclinations:

Most people thinking of pastoral ministry are excited to preach. I want to know if they are excited to preach at the rescue mission and excited to teach catechism to five-year-olds.

2.

Do I find myself stirred by good preaching?

If a man is called to preach the gospel he should be thrilled to hear it preached. The content should move him, and he should find himself thinking, "Oh, that I could proclaim this good news."

3.

Do I find myself stirred by bad preaching?

The last point was obvious. This one is less so, but just as important. I think there ought to be a fire in a man's bones when he hears the Word of God handled badly.

4.

Do I enjoy being around people?

Some pastors are extroverts; many are not. Whatever your personality, you won't be a good pastor if you don't like people and recoil from them as much as possible.

5.

Do I make friends easily?

This is a subjective test, but a lack of meaningful friendships is not a good sign. It could be an indication that you are too harsh, too much a loner or frankly too awkward to be effective in pastoral ministry.

6.

Do I like to read?

Thankfully there is no GPA or SAT requirement for pastoral ministry. And yet, if we are to be "apt to teach" we must be eager to learn. Preaching grows thin and ministry grows stale without time in the Book and the books.

There must be an aptness to teach and some measure of the other qualities needful for the office of a public instructor.

If a man be called to preach, he will be endowed with a degree of speaking ability, which he will cultivate and increase.

You must be fitted to lead, prepared to endure and able to persevere.

Mere ability to edify and aptness to teach is not enough, there must be other talents to complete the pastoral character. Sound judgment and solid experience must instruct you; gentle manners and loving affections must sway you; firmness and courage must be manifest; and tenderness and sympathy must not be lacking.

C.H. Spurgeon, similarly, had these things to say about the giftings of the pastor:

How do you measure up to the gifts listed by Luther, Spurgeon, Calvin and DeYoung?

Now there are varieties
of gifts, but the same Spirit;
and there are varieties
of service, but the same Lord;
and there are varieties of
activities, but it is the same
God who empowers them all in
everyone. To each is given the
manifestation of the Spirit for
the common good.

1 CORINTHIANS 12:4-7

What are some of the gifts you naturally possess? What are some of your spiritual gifts?

AFFIR

MATIONS —

Do others agree?

Unfortunately, most people lack an objective view of their own gifts and abilities. That's where the local church comes in. The second part of your evaluation is to consult trusted friends and church members who can speak to you honestly about your gifts and abilities. If they love you, they'll be honest with you. Remember, "faithful are the wounds of a friend, profuse are the kisses of an enemy" (Prov 27:6). An honest assessment of your gifts may be discouraging, but it's God's kindness that you be aware of your weaknesses.

You should also consult a trusted pastor. The apostle Paul told Timothy, "what you have heard from me in the presence of many witnesses entrust to faithful men who will be able to teach others also" (2 Tim 2:2). Pastors are called to recognize the gifts of others in the body whom God may be calling to ministry and to entrust the gospel to them. Plus, nobody knows the demands and daily life of the ministry better than those currently in it.

Lastly, God doesn't give people abilities so that they can enjoy those gifts alone. Rather, he gives gifts and abilities "for the common good" (1 Cor 12:8), and all gifts should be exercised "for building up" (1 Cor 14:26). It is vital that someone considering ministry honestly evaluate whether God appears to be using those gifts for the sake of the church.

Name other people who think you should pursue vocational ministry. In what contexts have they affirmed your ministry? What did they say?

The most important call is the objective call
of your church encouraging you to pursue
pastoral ministry.

KEVIN DEYOUNG

"I was made to see that the Holy Ghost never intended that men who have gifts and abilities should bury them in the earth, but rather did command and stir up such to the exercise of their gift."

JOHN BUNYAN

"I had sooner accept the opinion of a company of the Lord's people than my own upon so personal a subject as my own gifts and graces."

C.H. SPURGEON

Have these trusted friends, pastors and church members affirmed your gifts or voiced caution?

For by the grace given
to me I say to everyone
among you not to think
of himself more highly than
he ought to think, but to think
with sober judgment, each
according to the measure of faith
that God has assigned.

ROMANS 12:3

Do people benefit from your ministry? When you minister from the Word of God and serve in the church, do people often respond in ways that verify your calling? What ministry experiences seem to confirm your call?

Surely it were better to be a mud-raker, or a chimney-sweep, than to stand in the ministry as an utterly barren tree. The meanest occupation confers some benefit upon mankind, but the wretched man who occupies a pulpit and never glorifies his God by conversions is a blank, a blog, an eyesore, a mischief.

C.H. SPURGEON

WHAT NOW ?

BY DONALD S. WHITNEY

A call to preach is a call to prepare. Would you want a physician who'd had no preparation? Preparation is even more important for a physician of souls. Develop your spiritual disciplines, especially those of the Word and prayer. Devote yourself to your local church. Find a place to teach there. Study the Bible and theology as much as you can. Seriously consider enrolling in a solid seminary. When I told my dad (a layman) that God was calling me, he wisely advised, "If you can do anything else and be happy, do it." He was right. But I had to exclaim with the apostle Paul, "I am under compulsion; for woe is me if I do not preach the gospel" (1 Cor 9:16). All along God knew better than I the path that was most joyful for me.

Perhaps, after reading all that has come before, you still feel called to ministry, but you're not sure if the pastorate is for you. Maybe you're called to be an overseas missionary, or a church planter or maybe there's another role in the local church that suits your gifts.

Anyone who is sure of God's call will be concerned to achieve the best kind of preparation.

DEREK PRIME AND ALISTAIR BEGG

"I can now see clearly, that at the time I would first have gone out, though my intention was, I hope, good in the main — yet I overrated myself, and had not that spiritual judgment and experience which are requisite for so great a service."

JOHN NEWTON

Called to missions

M. David Sills, author of *The Missionary Call: Find Your Place in God's Plan for the World,* describes the missionary call as a combination of:

1.
An awareness of the need for missions;

2.
An understanding of Christ's commands for missions;

3.
A passionate concern for the lost;

4.
A radical commitment to God;

5.
The blessing of the local church;

6.
The Spirit's gifting; and

7.
An indescribable yearning.

Called to church plant

Jim Stitzinger, director of the Bevin Center for Missions Mobilization at Southern Seminary, describes the church planter's call as a combination of:

Exemplary character:
a Christ exalting life of prayer, integrity and humility;

Entrepreneurial capability:
a Christ-dependent boldness in servant leadership;

Earnest convictions:
an accurate theology that drives methodology and demonstrates biblical imperatives;

Endurance capacity:
a relentless work ethic and Christlike ability to withstand trials and criticism;

Evangelistic compulsion:
a continual instinct to press toward unbelievers with the gospel;

Equipping competence:
an ability to disciple, delegate and deploy believers into gospel ministry; and

Effective communication:
clarity in articulating and uniting believers in both vision and mission;

Epic confidence:
a dogged determination to trust Christ to build his church in his time and in his way.

What kind of ministry do you see yourself doing?

How would you benefit from theological training?

"Do your best to present yourself to God as one approved, a worker who has no need to be ashamed, rightly handling the word of truth. ... So flee youthful passions and pursue righteousness, faith, love and peace, along with those who call on the Lord from a pure heart. Have nothing to do with foolish, ignorant controversies; you know that they breed quarrels. And the Lord's servant must not be quarrelsome but kind to everyone, able to teach, patiently enduring evil, correcting his opponents with gentleness."

2 TIMOTHY 2:15, 22-25

"The scriptural qualifications of the ministry do, indeed, involve the idea of knowledge ... of God and his plan of salvation. He who has not this knowledge is incapable of preaching the Word of God. But he who knows it, not superficially, not merely in those plain and simple declarations known to every believing reader, but in the power as revealed in its precious and sanctifying doctrines, is fitted to bring forth out of his treasure things new and old, and is a workman that needeth not to be ashamed."

JAMES PETIGRU BOYCE

MINISTRY TODAY

BY R. ALBERT MOHLER JR.

The gospel ministry has always had challenges; just look at the lives of the apostles. There's no reason to think those challenges will go anywhere soon. Today's gospel ministers, missionaries and Christian leaders will face every one of those challenges, and then some new ones. Virtually every day of his life, the gospel minister will serve in a context of constant challenges to gospel truth and to biblical authority. Many of these challenges will come with an invitation, or perhaps a demand, that the Christian leader compromise his convictions and join the moral revolution that is undeniably taking place.

This kind of compromise is precisely what biblical Christians cannot do. When the opportunity comes to compromise what Scripture says — and the opportunity will come for each of us — the only way to respond is with conviction, with clarity and with grace. Striking such a balance requires the Christian minister to think strategically about what it means to speak truthfully and lovingly to a society that increasingly sees us as the moral outlaws. But abandoning the truth of God's Word is not an option. This holds true for individual Christians, and it holds true for theological institutions.

As a theological institution, Southern Seminary — and its undergraduate school, Boyce College — is relentless about the task of training this generation of gospel ministers to stand firm as ambassadors of the gospel, preaching it in churches and taking it to the ends of the earth. We know what kind of world it is into which we send our graduates, and we are aware of the demands the world will make on them, but Southern Seminary and Boyce College will go to whatever lengths needed to make sure that this generation of Christian ministers and missionaries is prepared.

> When you come,
> bring the cloak that
> I left with Carpus at
> Troas, also the
> books, and above all
> the parchments.
>
> 2 TIMOTHY 4:13

> He is inspired, and yet he wants books! He
> has been preaching at least for thirty years,
> and yet he wants books! He had seen the
> Lord, and yet he wants books! ... The
> apostle says to Timothy and so he says to
> every preacher, "Give thyself unto reading."
>
> C.H. SPURGEON

RECOMMENDED RESOURCES

Brothers, We Are Not Professionals, John Piper

Church Planter: The Man, the Message, the Mission, Darrin Patrick

The Conviction to Lead: 25 Principles for Leadership that Matters, R. Albert Mohler Jr.

The Cross and Christian Ministry, D.A. Carson

Dangerous Calling: Confronting the Unique Challenges of Pastoral Ministry, Paul David Tripp

A Guide to Expository Ministry, Daniel S. Dumas, ed.

He Is Not Silent: Preaching in a Postmodern World, R. Albert Mohler Jr.

Lectures to My Students, C.H. Spurgeon

The Missionary Call: Find Your Place in God's Plan for the World, M. David Sills

Nine Marks of a Healthy Church, Mark Dever

Preaching and Preachers, D. Martyn Lloyd-Jones

Preaching: How to Preach Biblically, John MacArthur

Shepherds After My Own Heart, Timothy Laniak

CONTRIBUTORS

R. ALBERT MOHLER JR. is the ninth president of The Southern Baptist Theological Seminary, where he also serves as a professor of Christian theology. Mohler is the author of *Conviction to Lead: 25 Principles for Leadership that Matters, He is Not Silent, Culture Shift, Desire and Deceit* and several other books. Mohler hosts two podcasts: "The Briefing," and "Thinking in Public." He also writes a popular blog with regular commentary on moral, cultural and theological issues, all of which can be accessed at www.AlbertMohler.com. Mohler is an ordained minister, and has served as pastor and staff minister of several Southern Baptist churches. He is married to Mary and has two children.

DONALD S. WHITNEY is associate professor of biblical spirituality at The Southern Baptist Theological Seminary. He is the founder and president of The Center for Biblical Spirituality. Prior to his ministry as a seminary professor, Whitney was pastor of Glenfield Baptist Church in Glen Ellyn, Ill., for almost 15 years. Altogether, he has served local churches in pastoral ministry for 24 years. He is the author of *Spiritual Disciplines for the Christian Life*. He is married to Caffy and has one daughter.

DANIEL S. DUMAS is a teaching pastor and elder at Crossing Church in Louisville, Ky. He is passionate about leadership, expository preaching, biblical manhood and being a transformational ministry architect. He is the co-author of *A Guide to Biblical Manhood* and editor of *A Guide to Expository Ministry*. Dumas became a senior vice president at Southern Seminary in October 2007. He came to Louisville from Grace Community Church in Sun Valley, Calif., where he served as elder, executive pastor, pastor of assimilation, director of conferences and pastor of the Cornerstone Fellowship Group. Prior to joining the staff at Grace, Dan logged extensive ministry hours at many local churches. He is married to Jane and has two children.

PRODUCTION

PROJECT EDITOR

MATT DAMICO is a staff writer for Southern Seminary. He earned a bachelor of arts in English from the University of Minnesota in 2008 before moving to Louisville, Ky. He graduated from Southern with a master of divinity in 2012, and currently serves as associate pastor of worship at Kenwood Baptist Church in Louisville. He is married to Anna.

DESIGNER

ANDREA STEMBER joined Southern Seminary's creative team in 2011 after working four years in the Chicago, Ill., graphic design scene. Though she loves the city, Andrea was born and raised in the state of Iowa, where she earned her bachelor of fine arts degree in graphic design from Iowa State University. She is married to Daniel, and they are the proud parents of Eleanor.

NOTES

Some of the questions included were provided by Southern Seminary professors Hershael W. York, Jeremy Pierre and Robert L. Plummer. RuthAnne Irvin, a writer at Southern Seminary, helped gather quotes. Material from Kevin DeYoung and John Piper was used with permission. Material on page 114 was adapted from *The Missionary Call: Find Your Place in God's Plan for the World*. Published by Moody Publishers, 2008, Chicago, IL. Used by permission.

SOUTHERN
SEMINARY

PREPARE
— FOR YOUR —
CALLING

If you're ready to take the step to prepare for ministry, visit our website for information about Southern Seminary and what it has to offer for your training and theological education.

To start an application, schedule a visit to campus or request more information, visit www.sbts.edu/apply.

If you have any questions, call Southern's admissions office at (502) 897-4200 or email admissions@sbts.edu.

If you're interested in undergraduate studies, check out Boyce College, the undergraduate school of Southern Seminary. For information on Boyce, visit **www.boycecollege.com**.

www.sbts.edu

2825 LEXINGTON RD. LOUISVILLE, KY 40280 | (502) 897-4200